MIND MAPPING NOTEBOOK

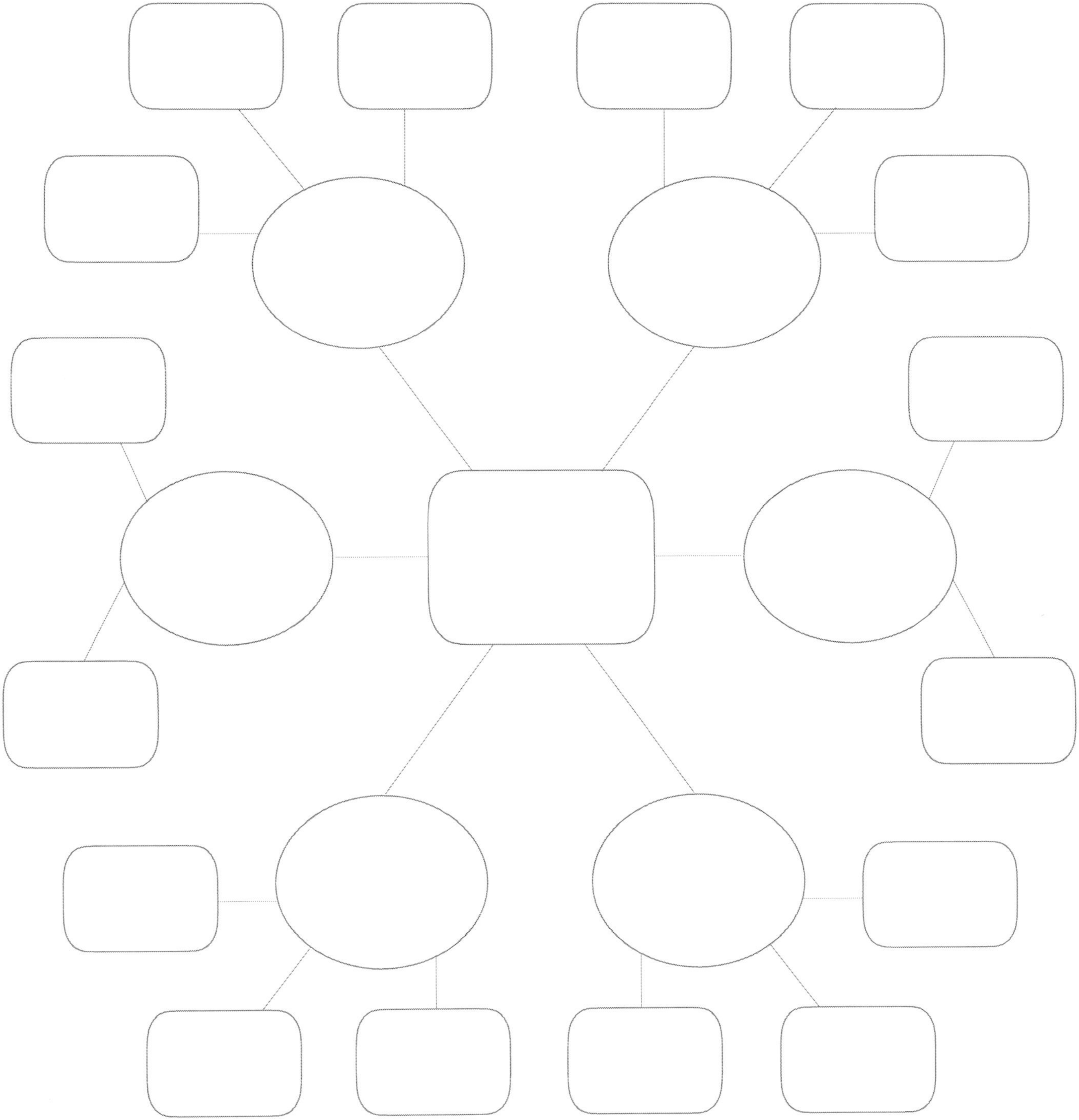

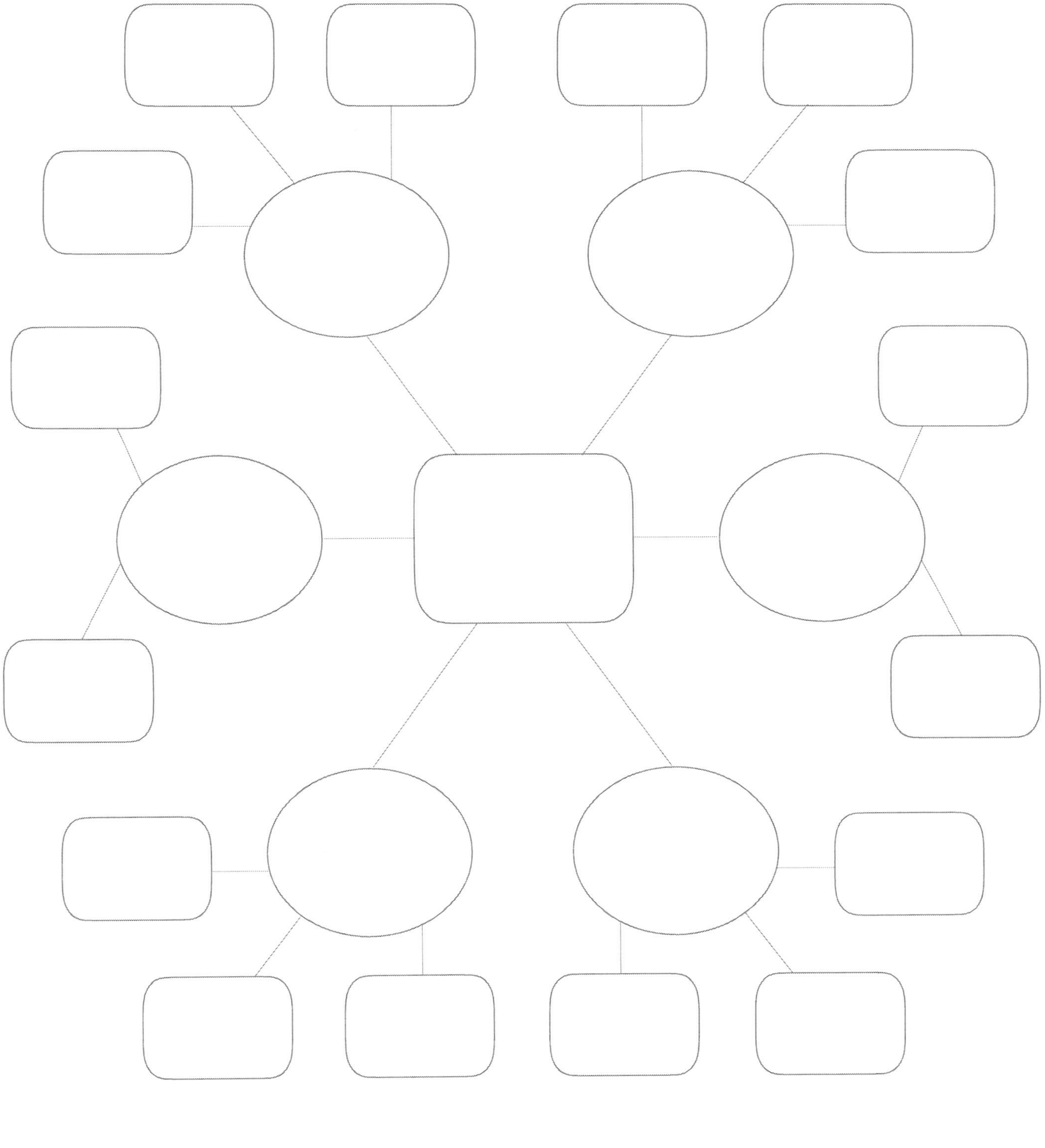

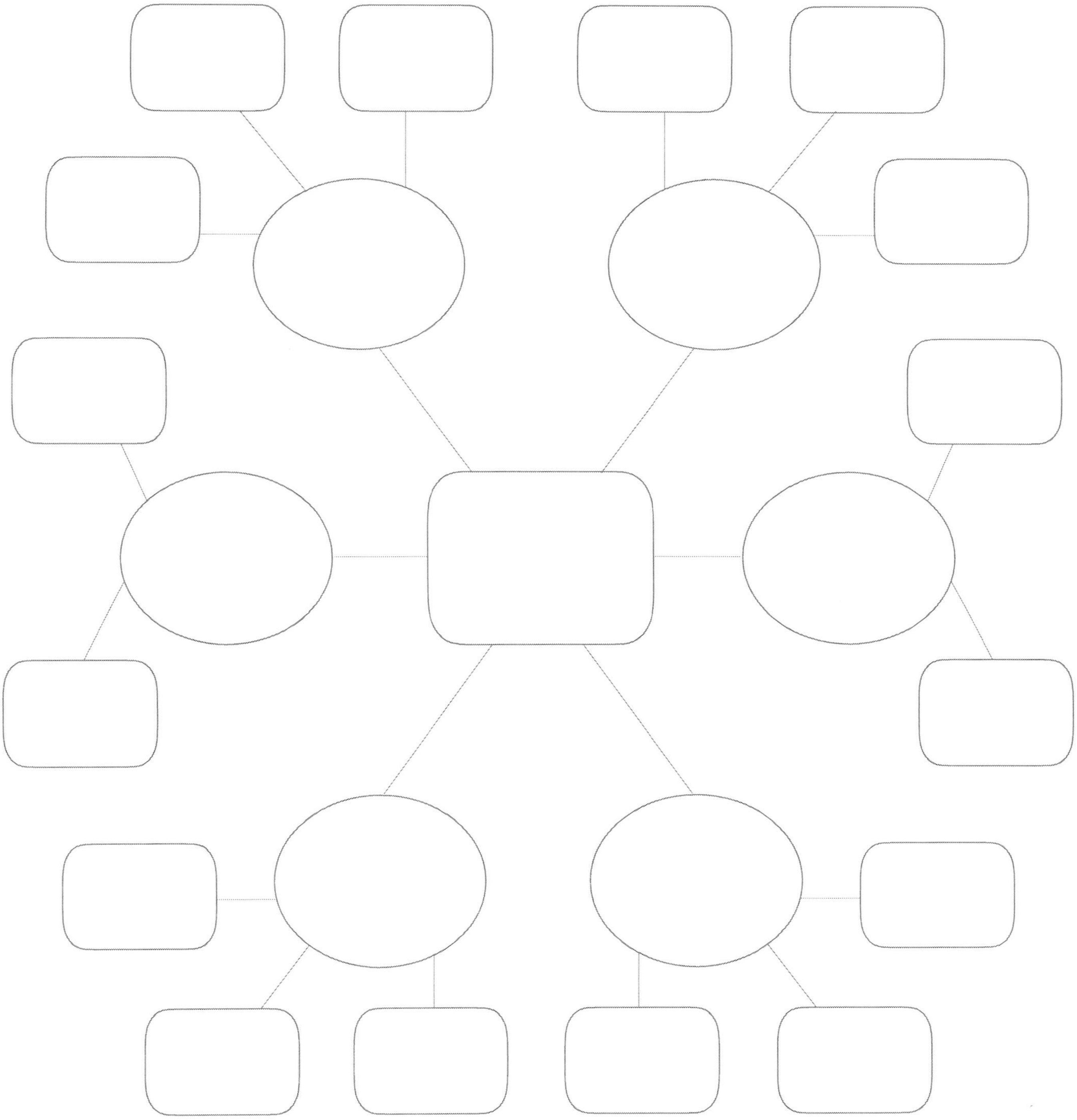

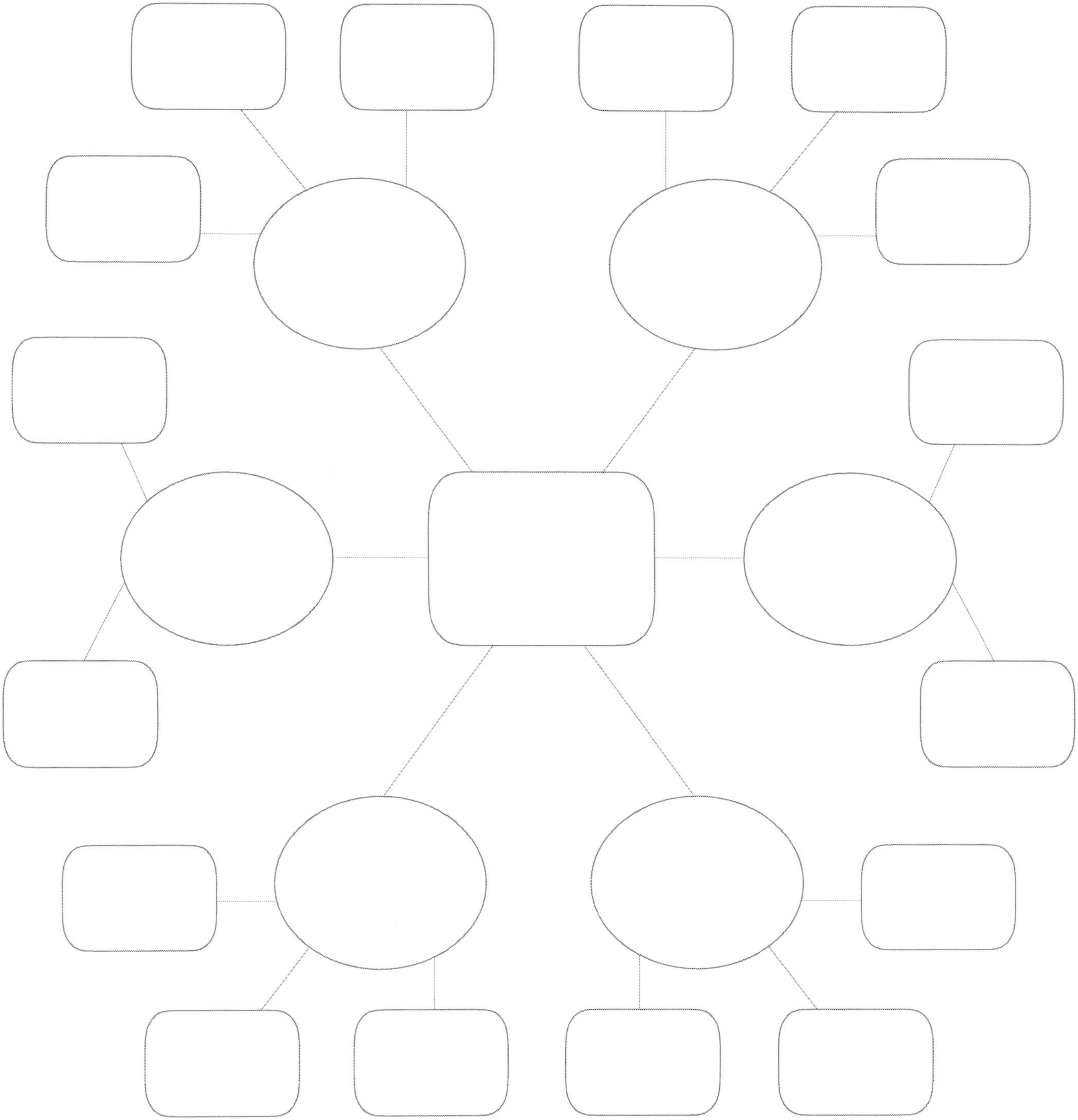

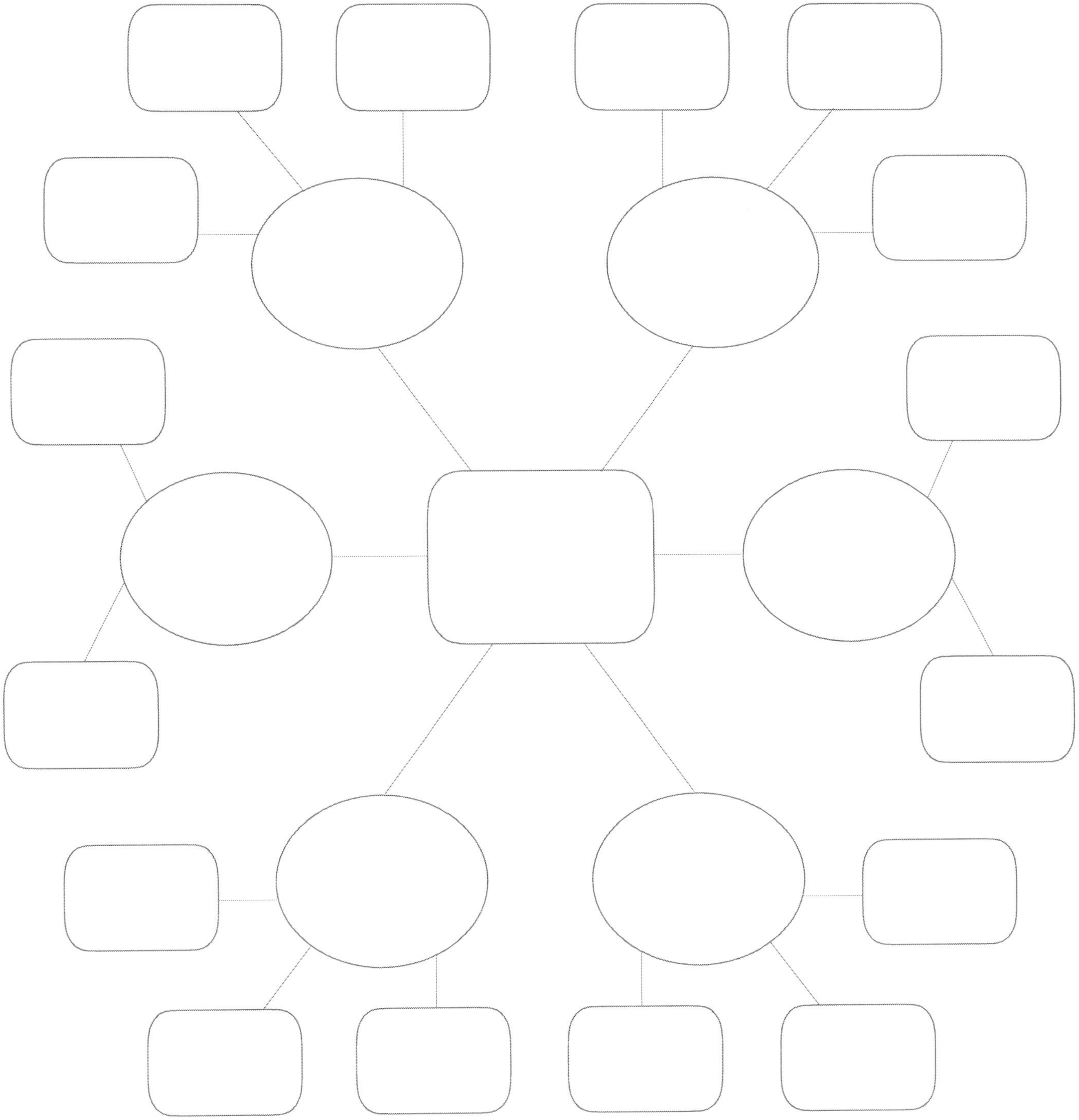

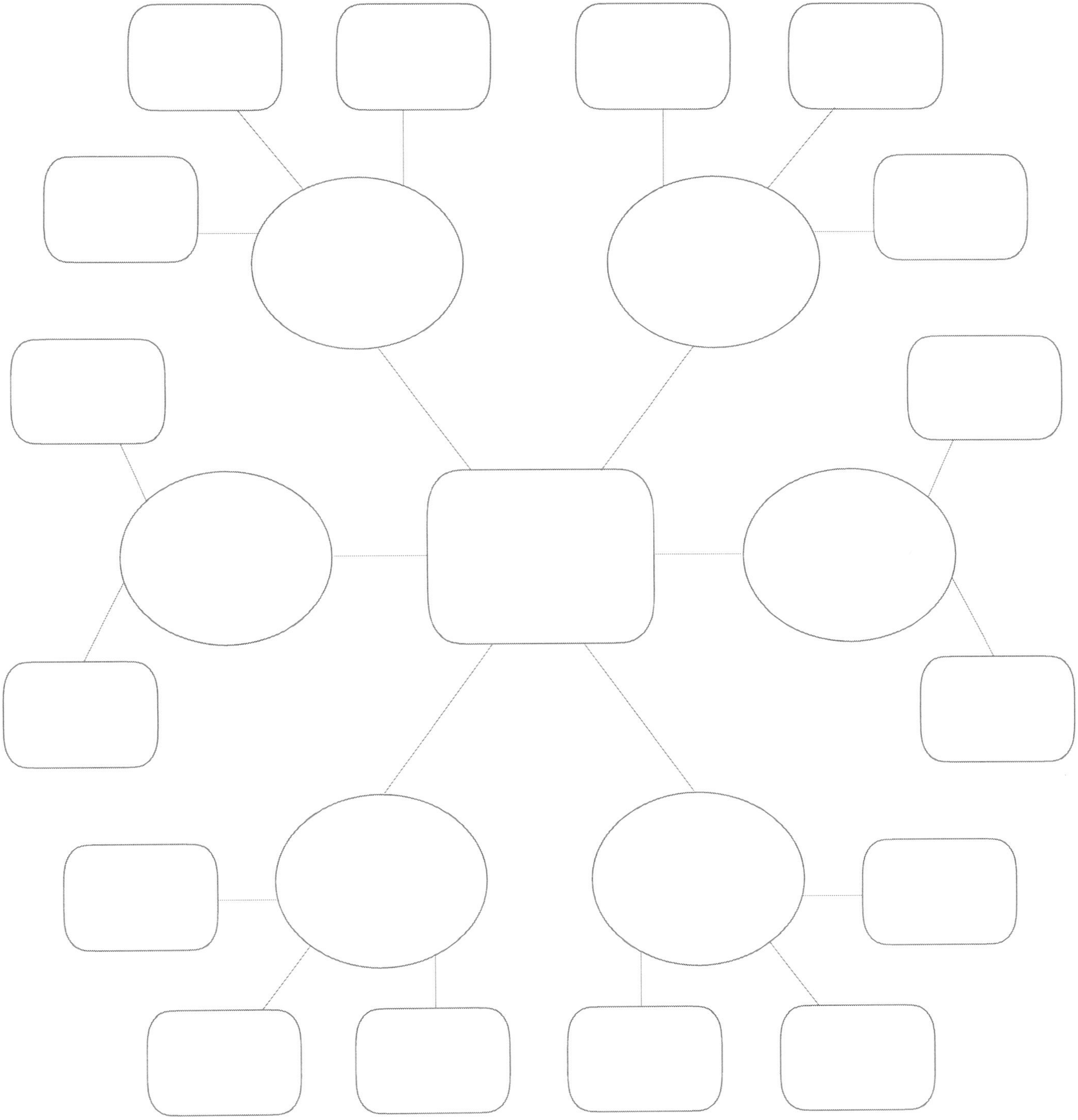

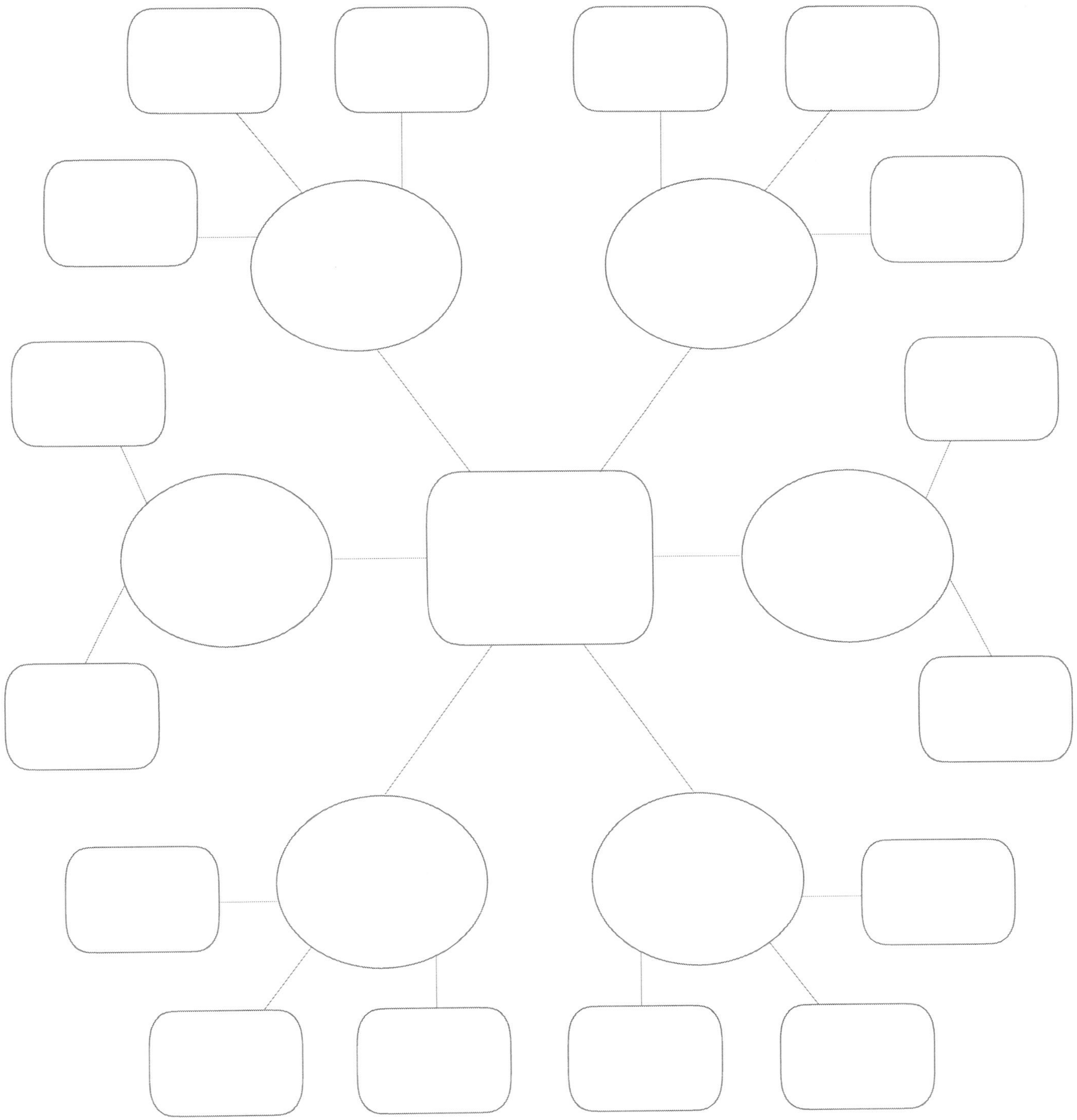

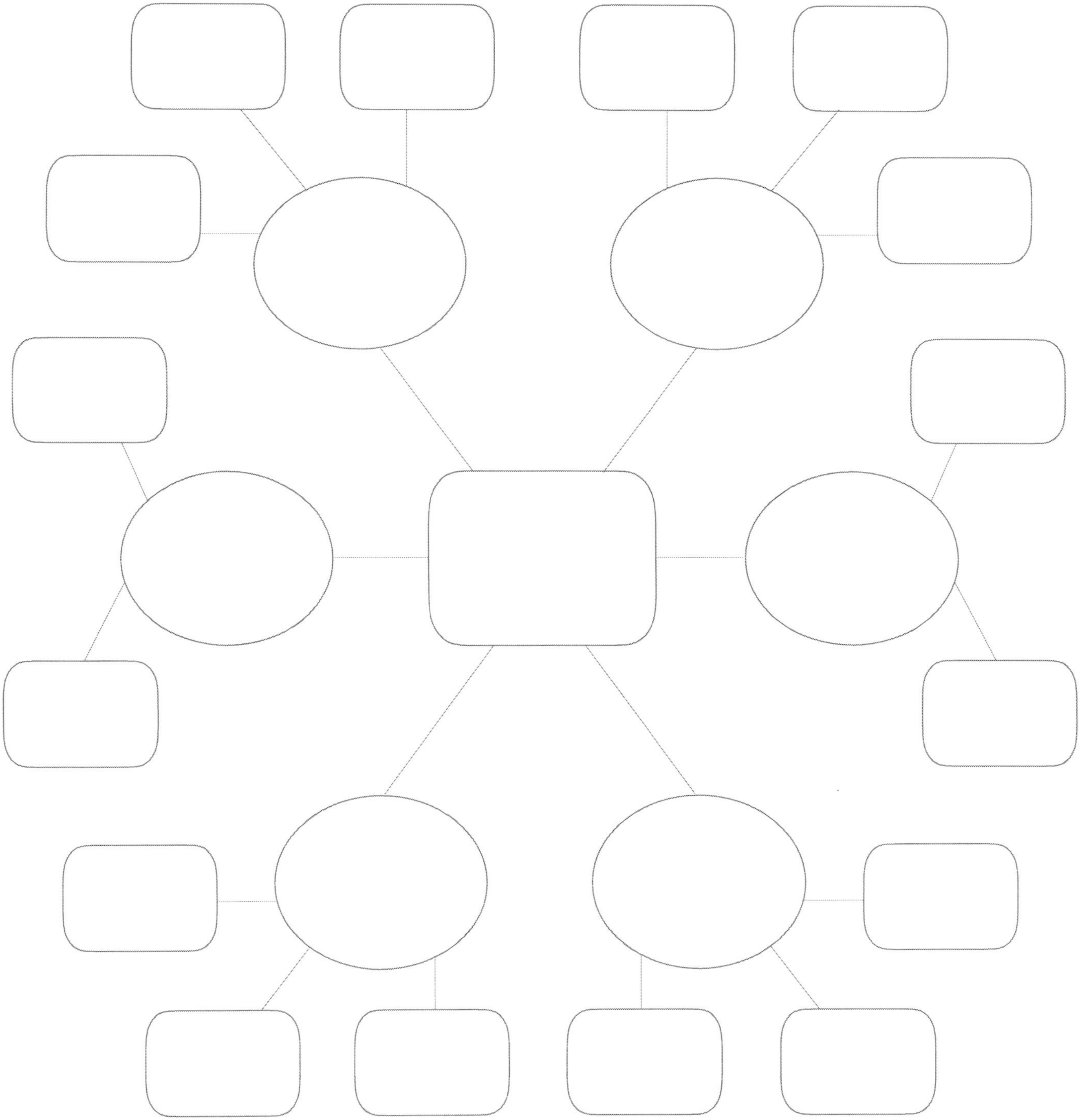

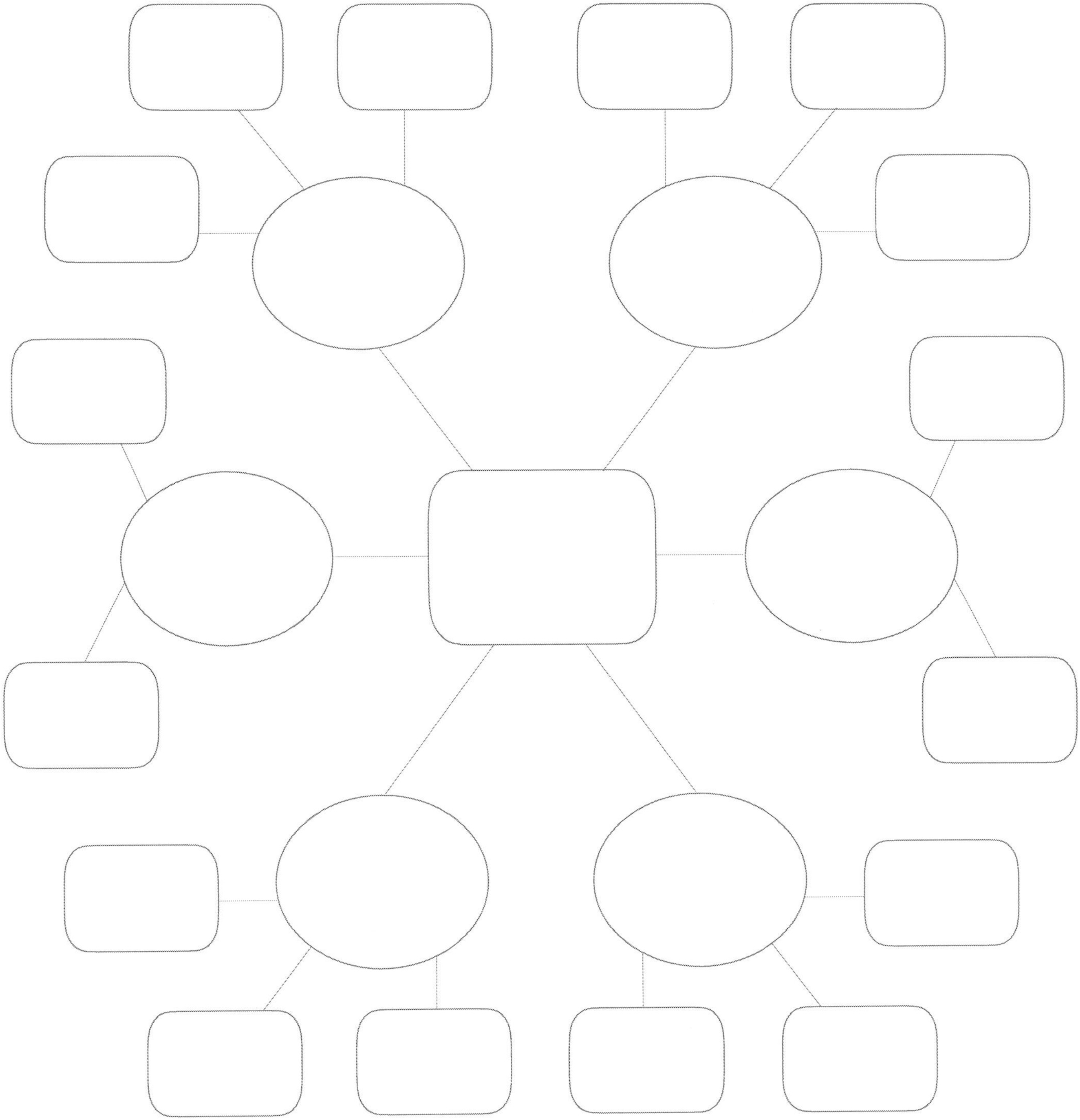

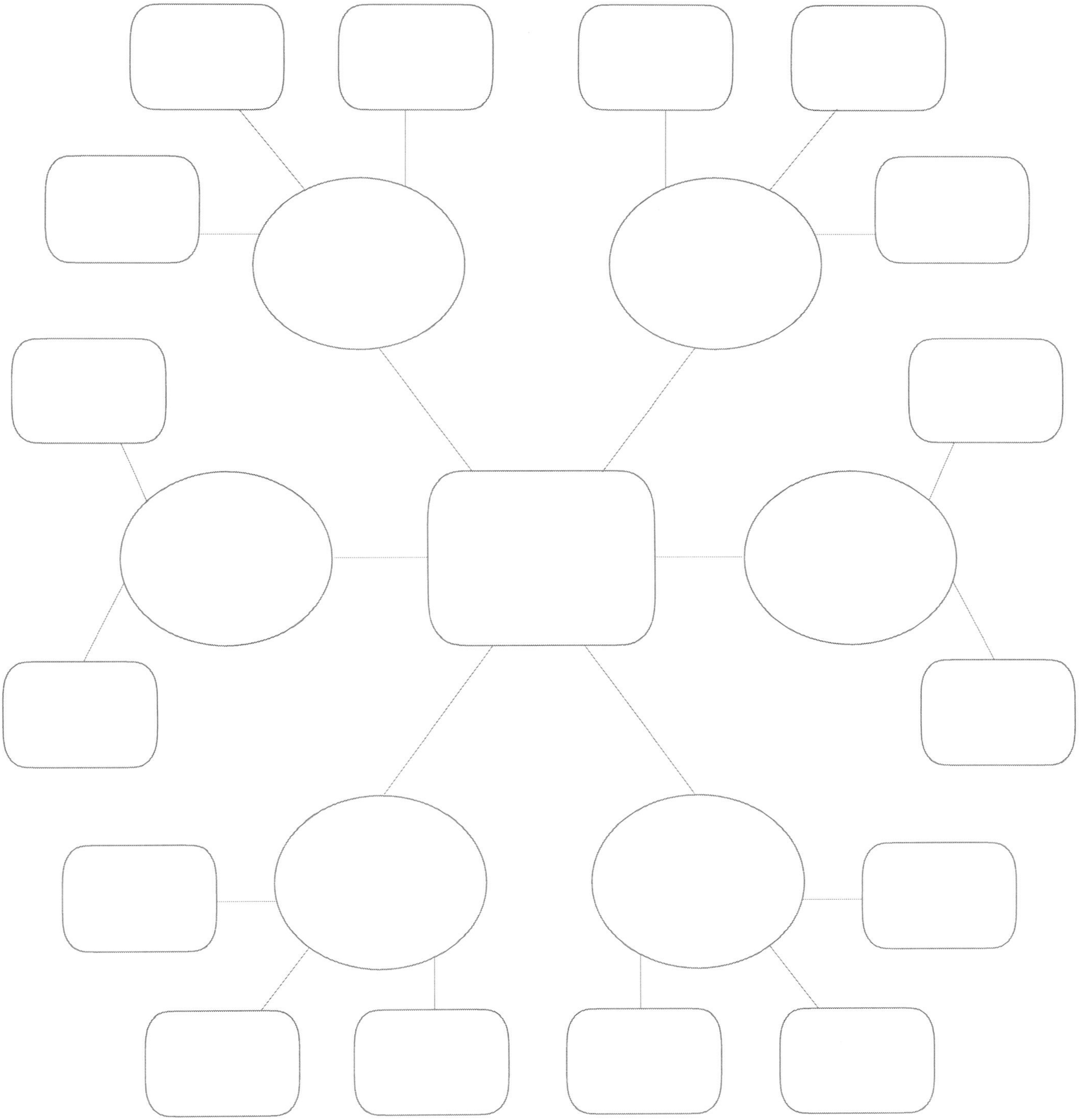

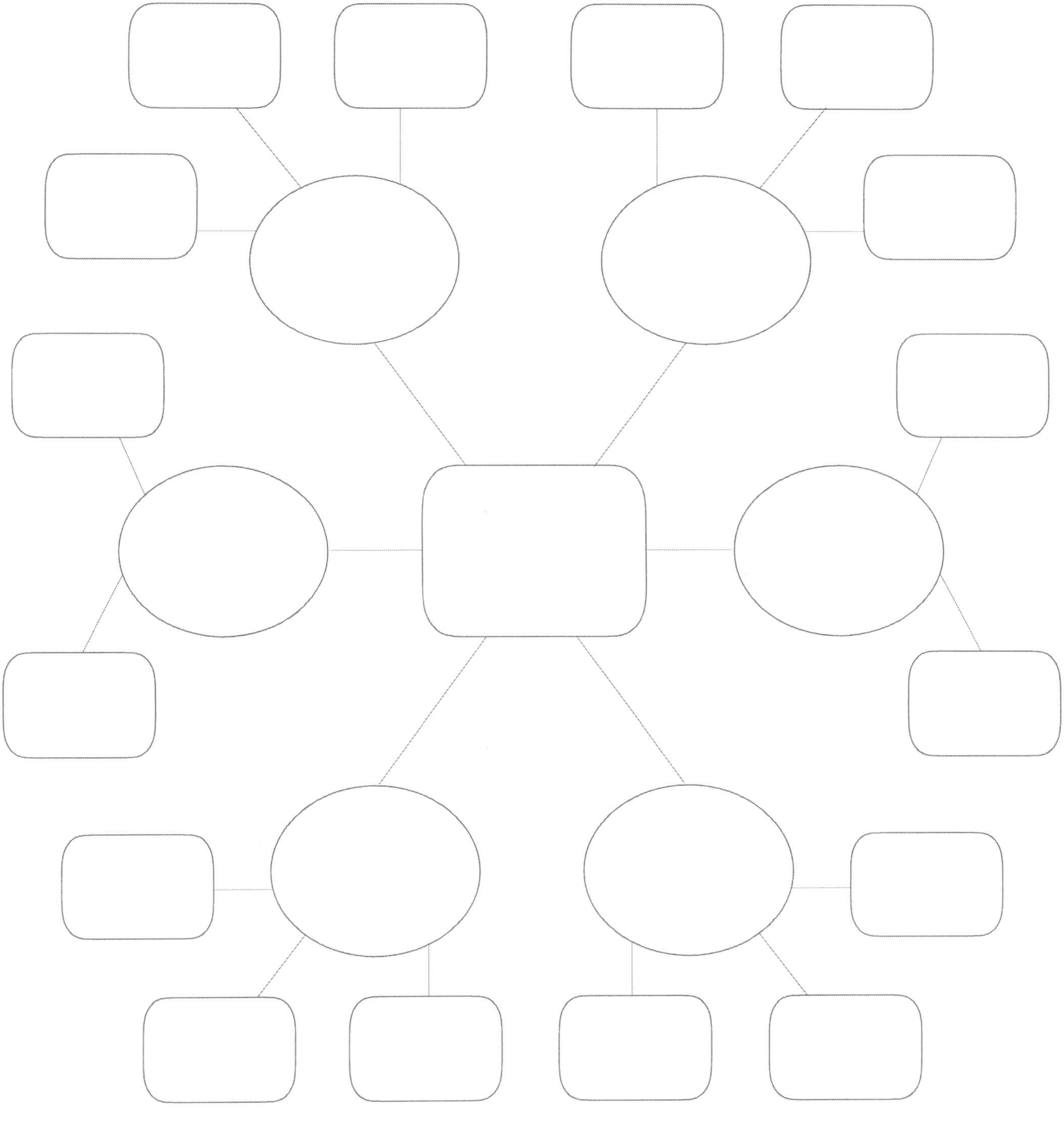

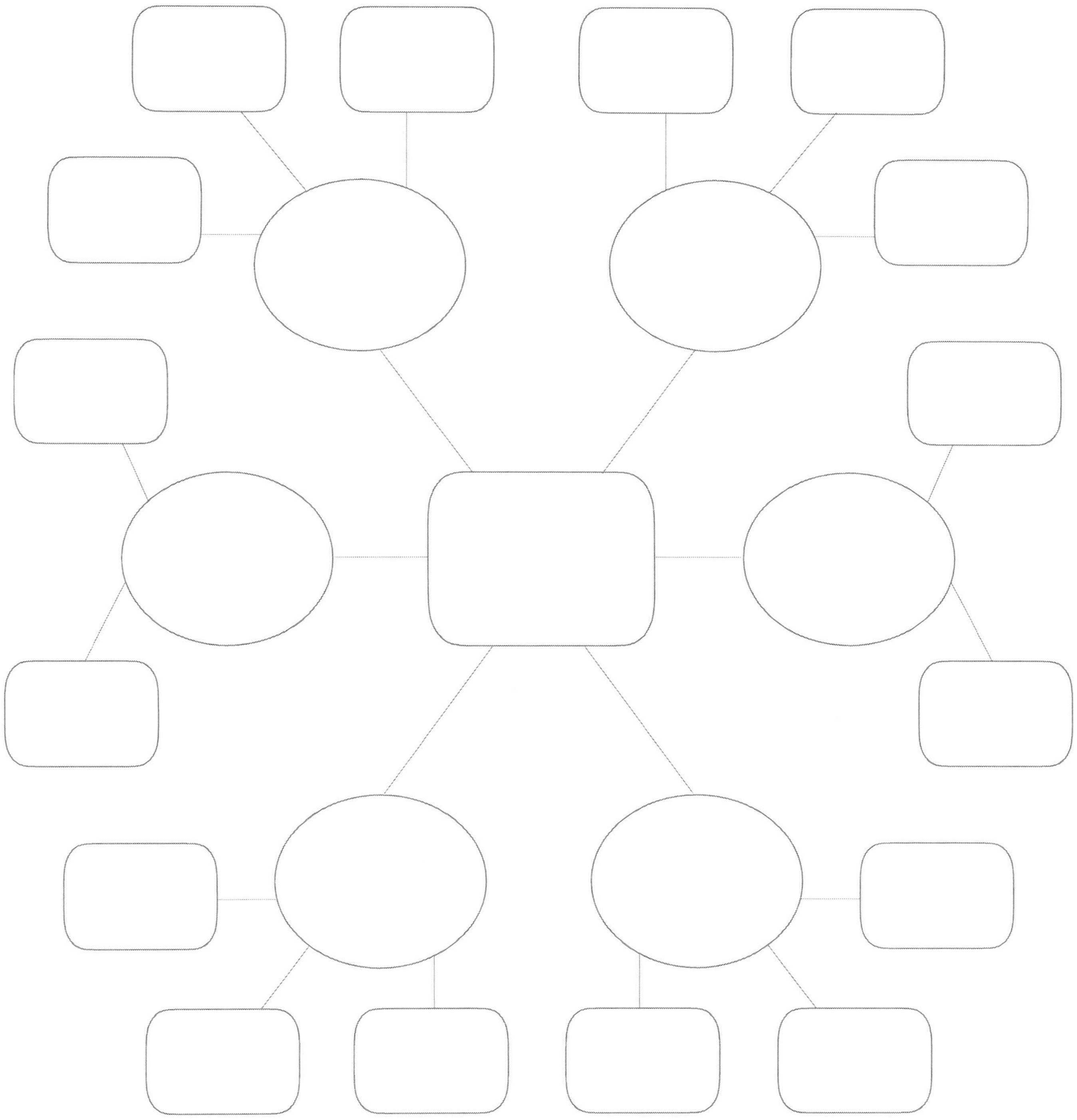

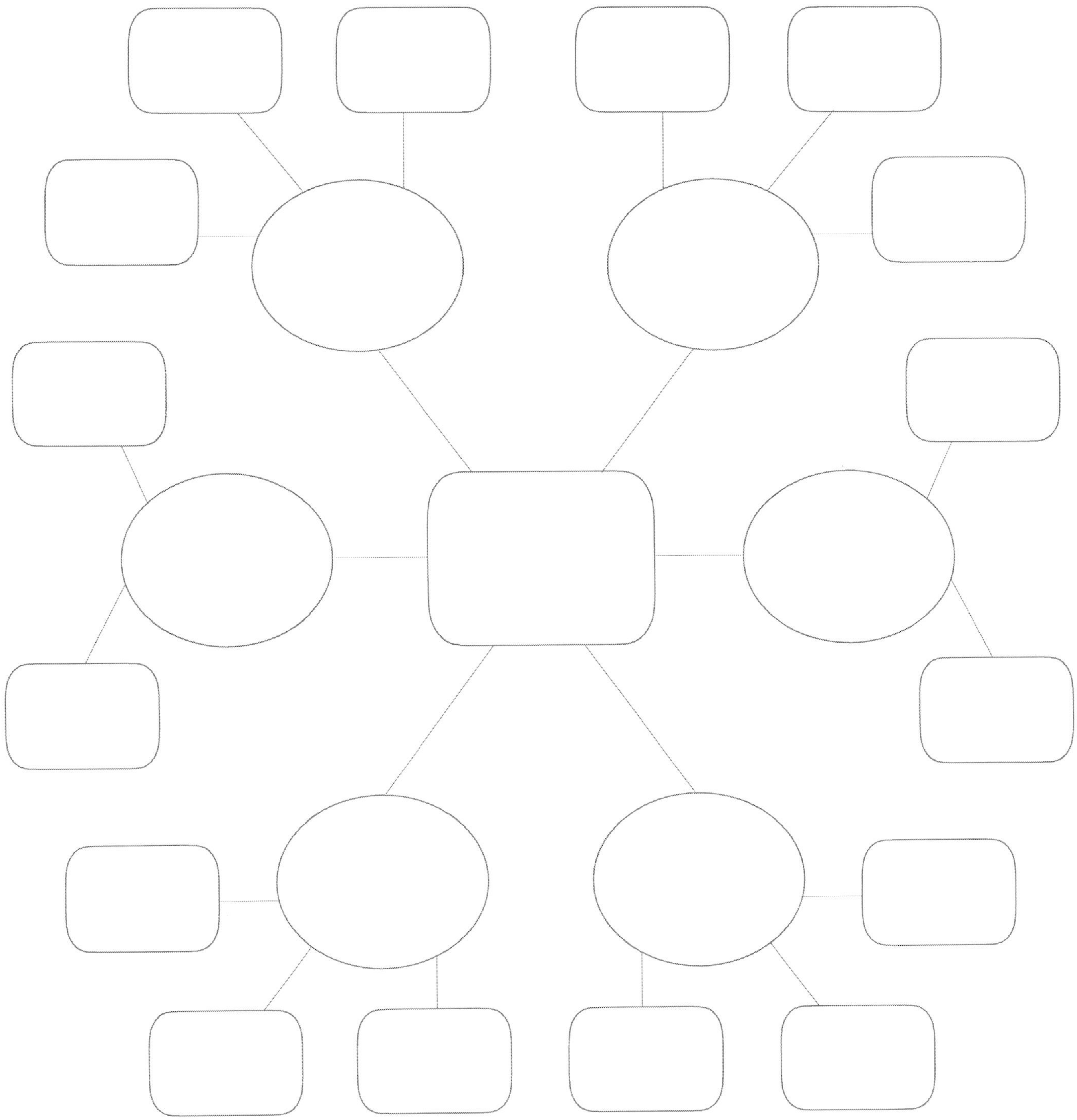

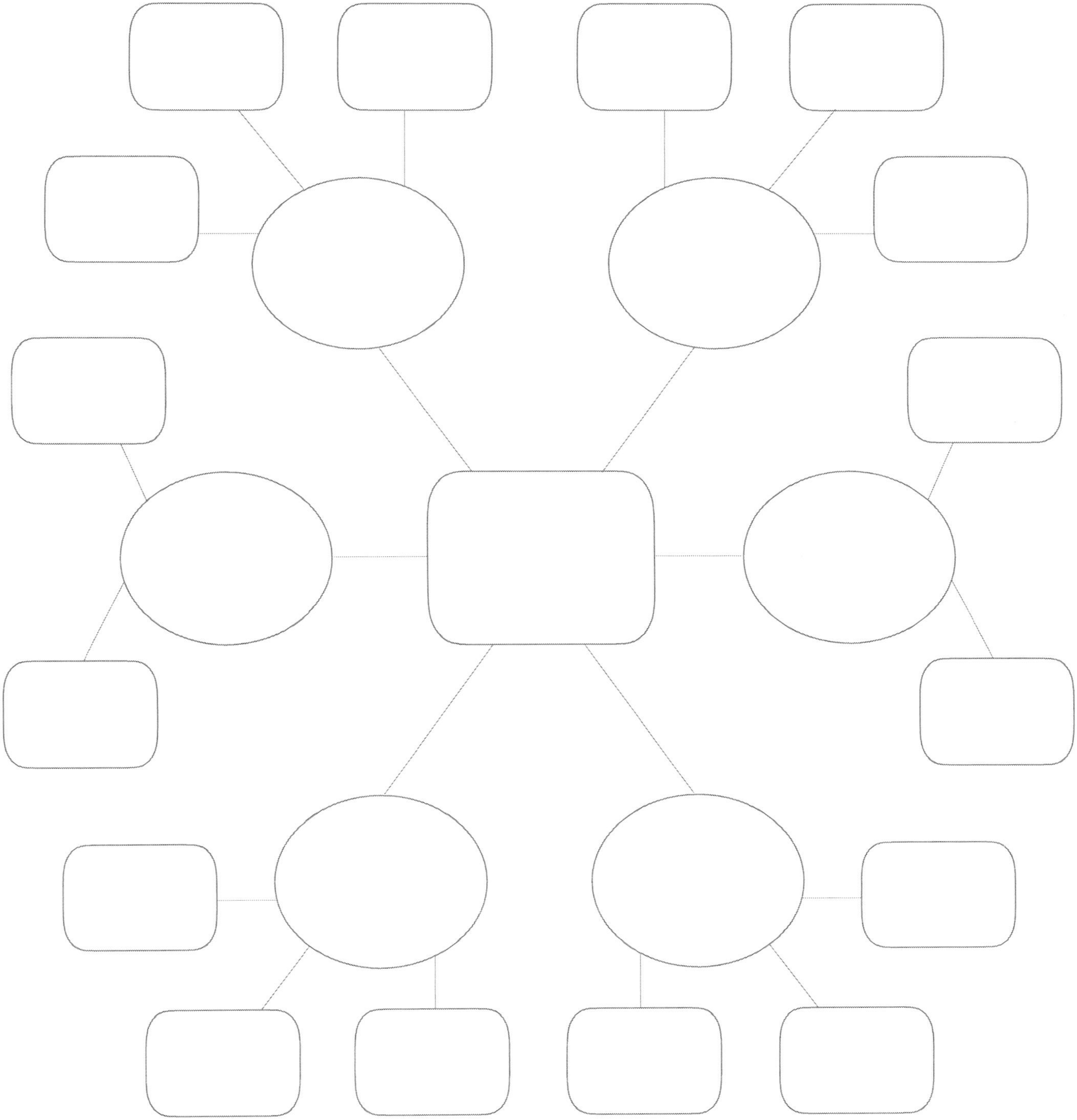

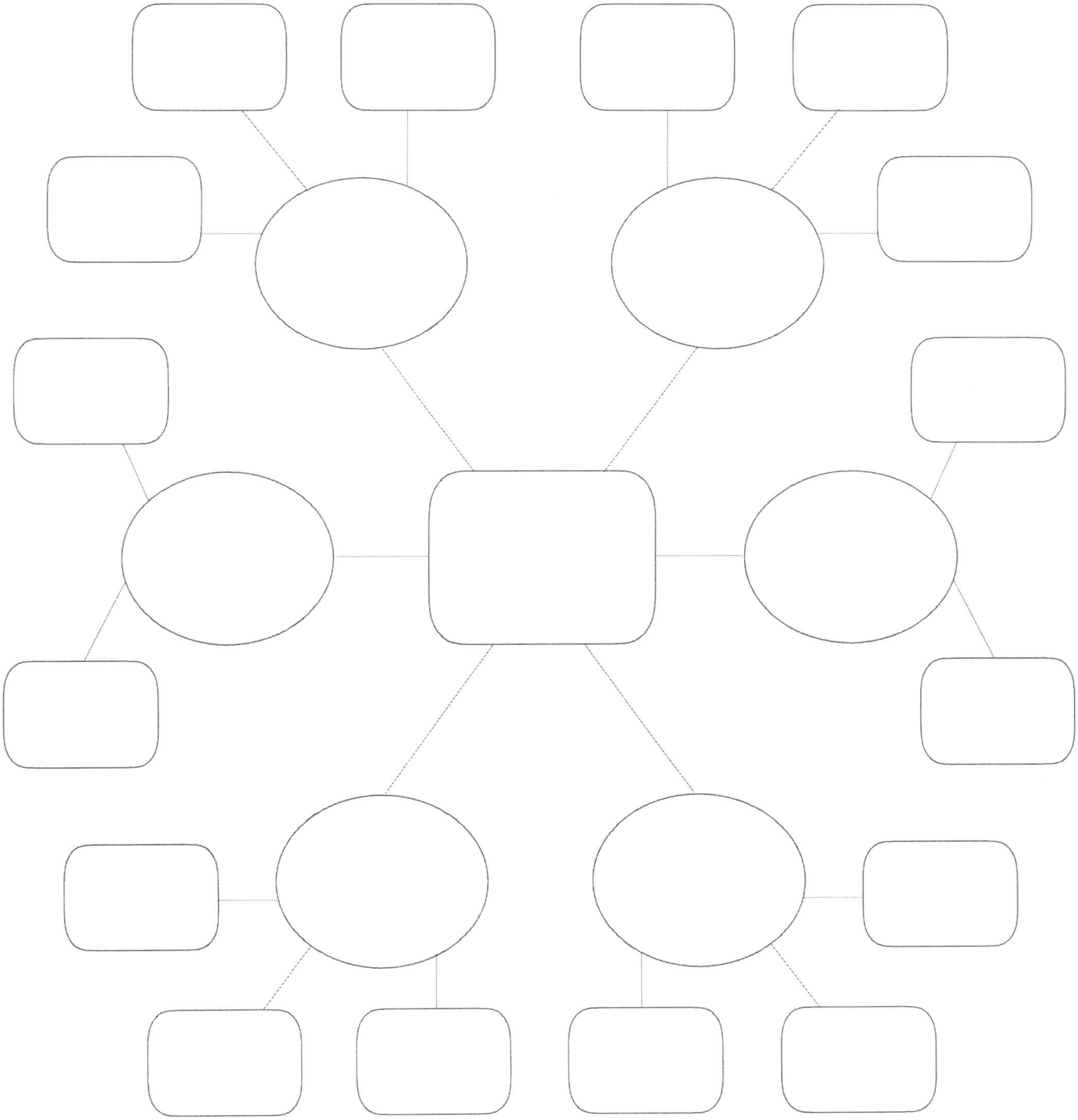

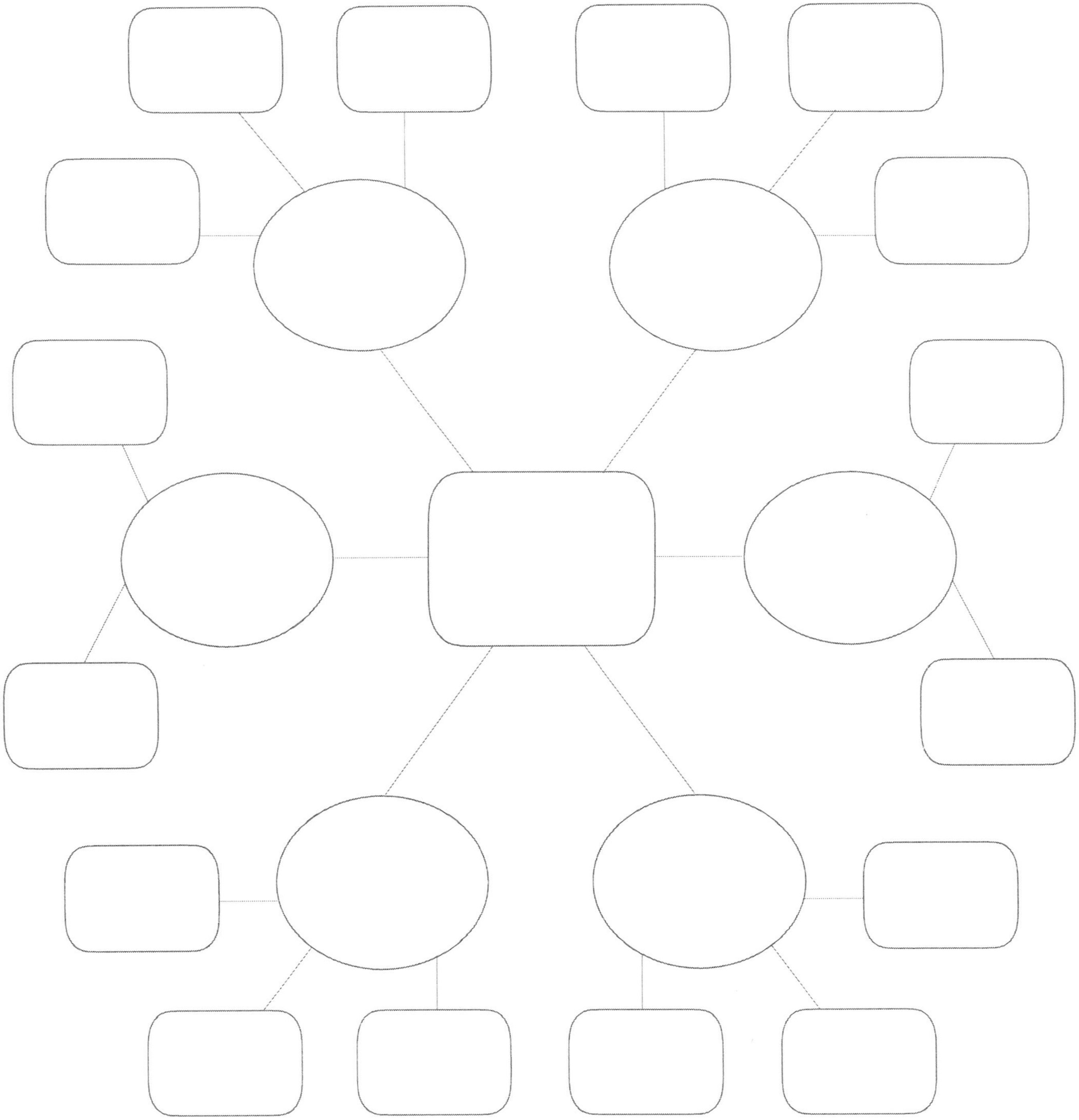

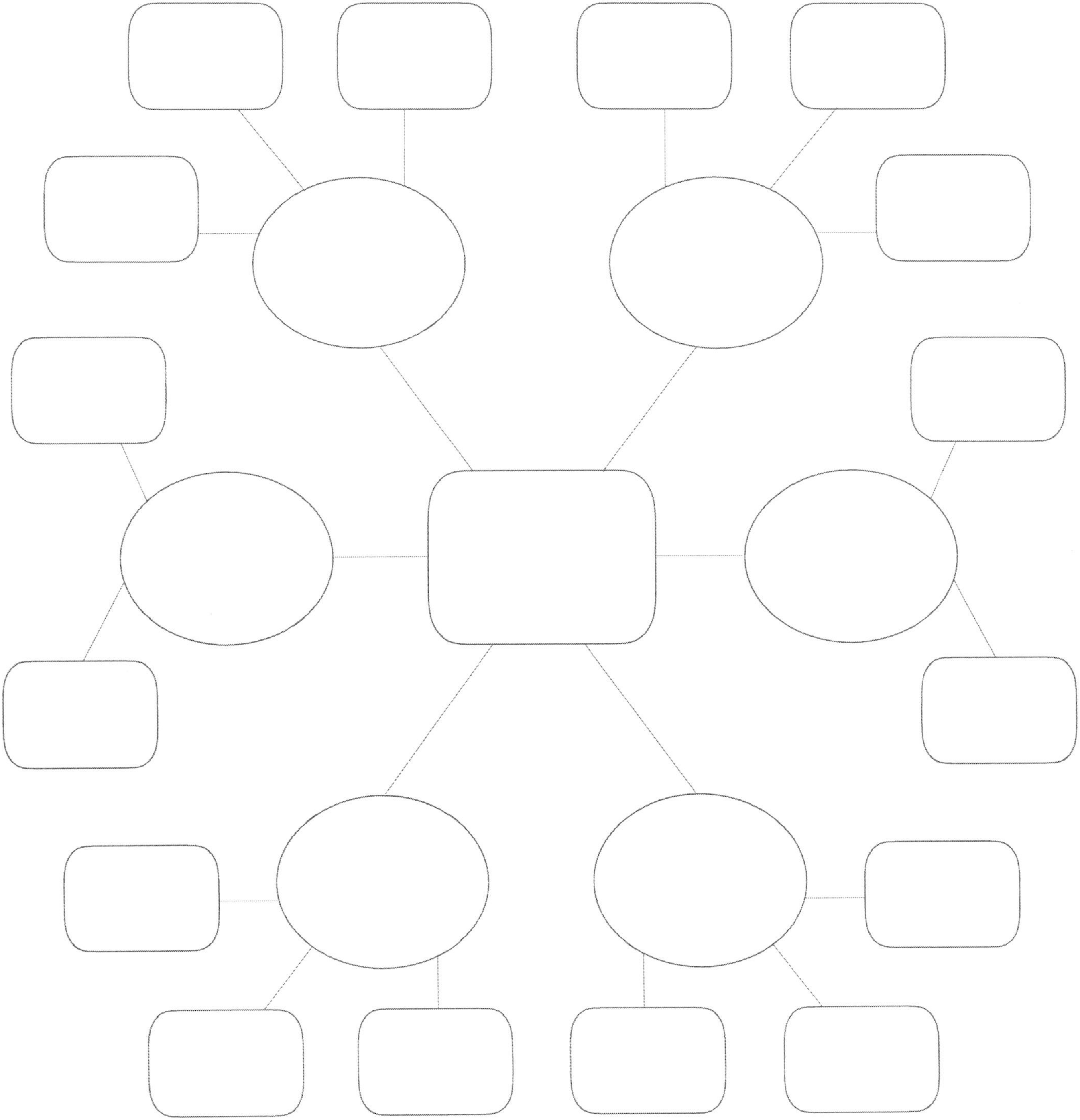

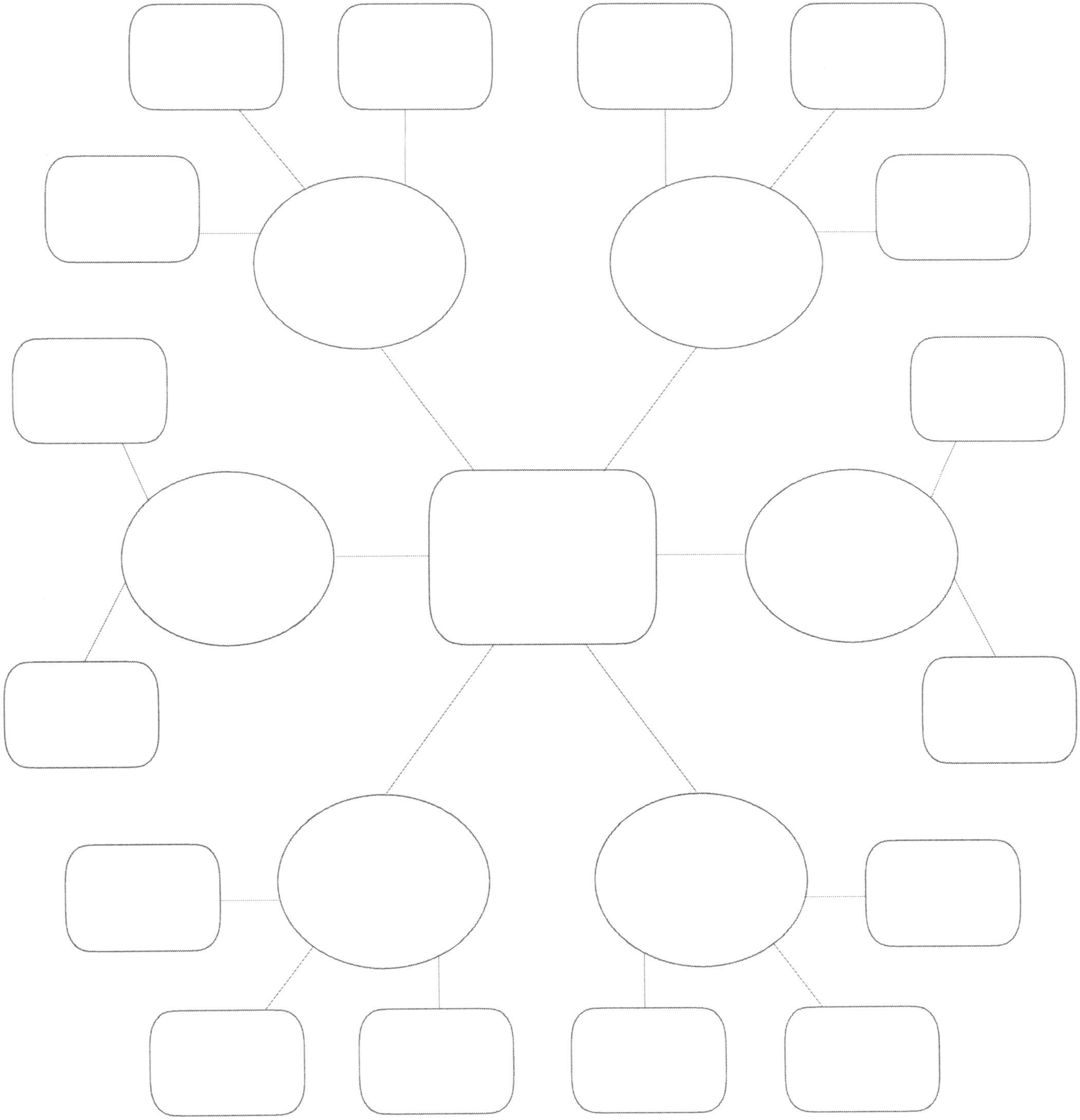

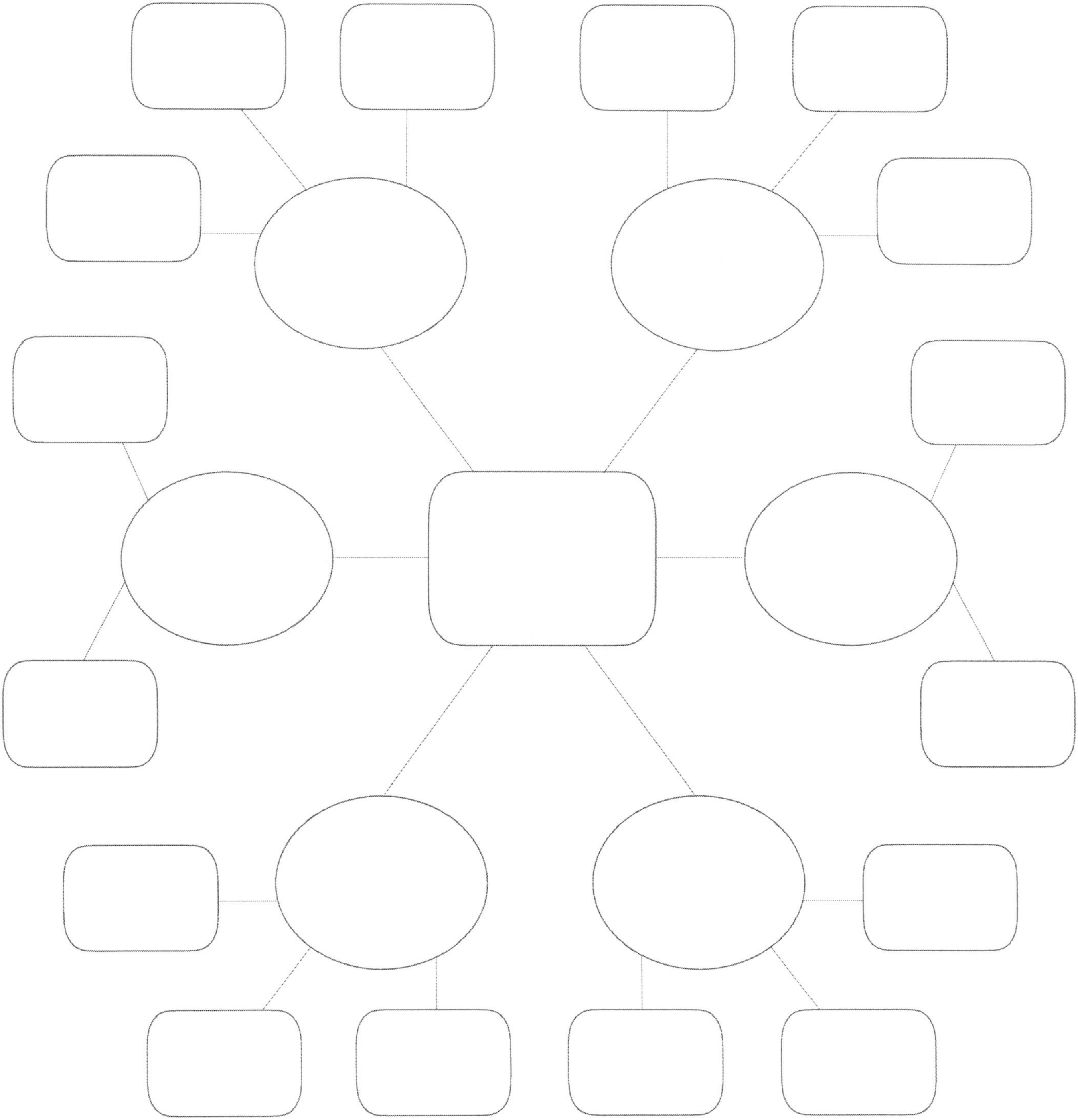

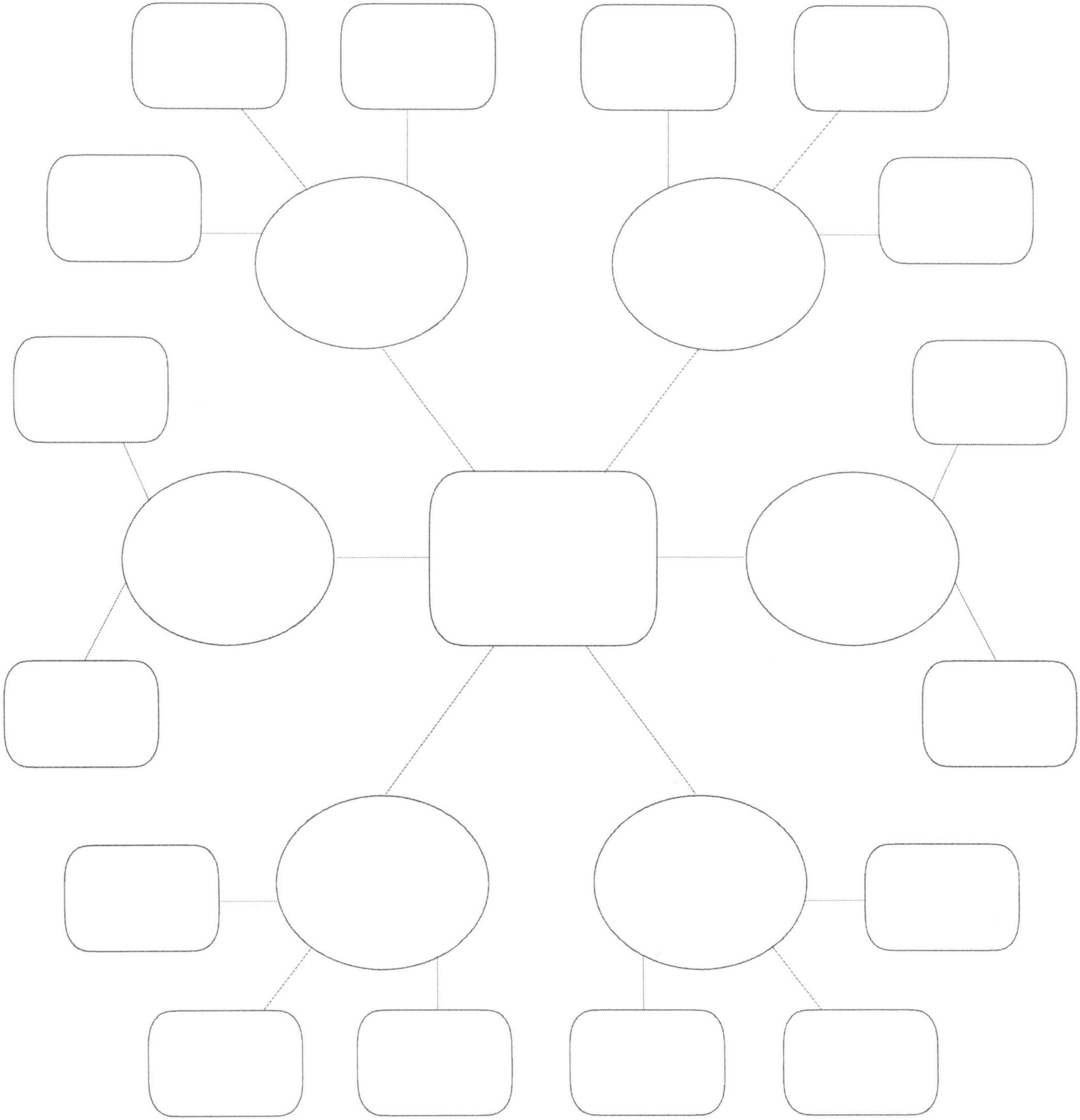

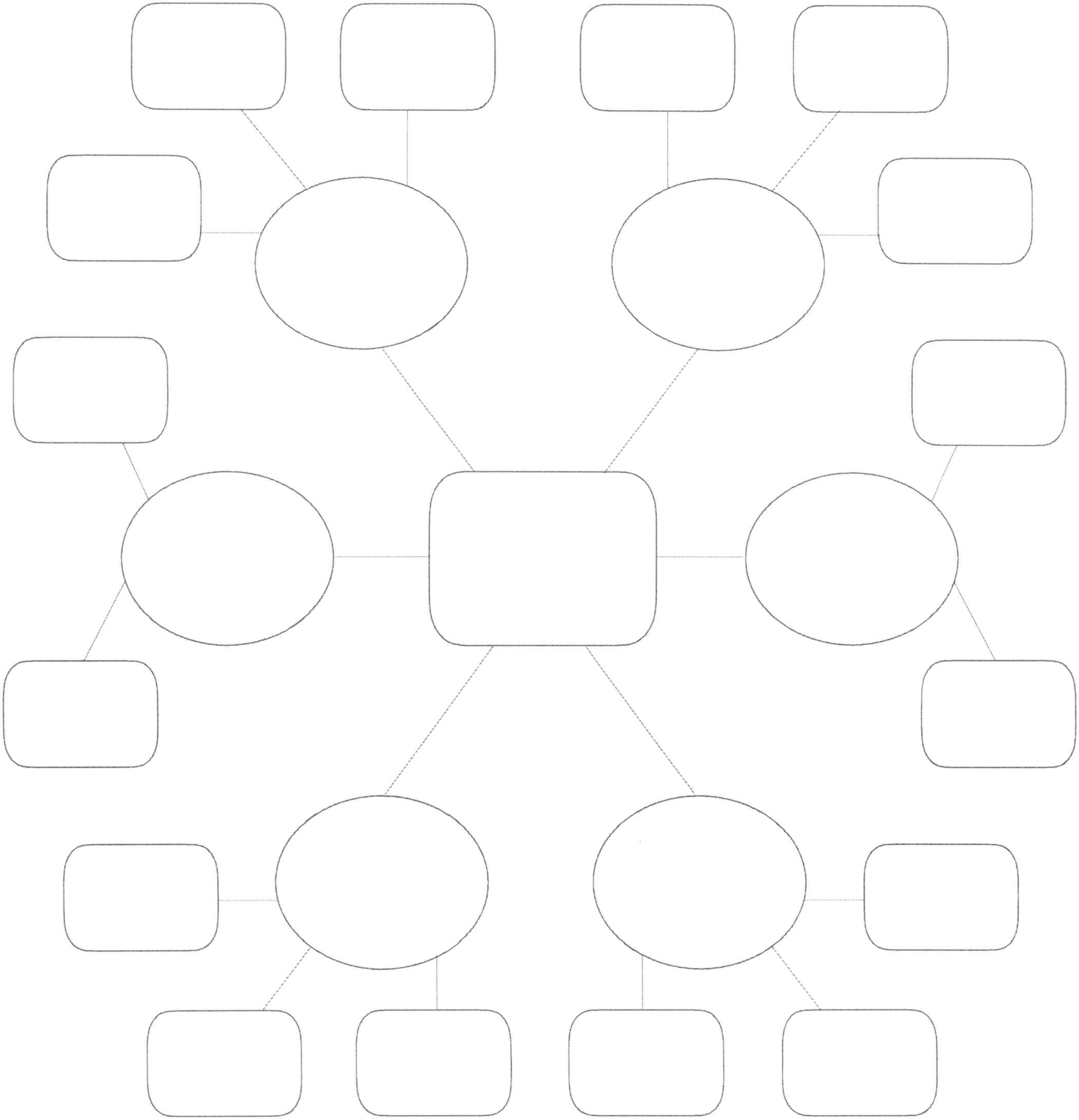

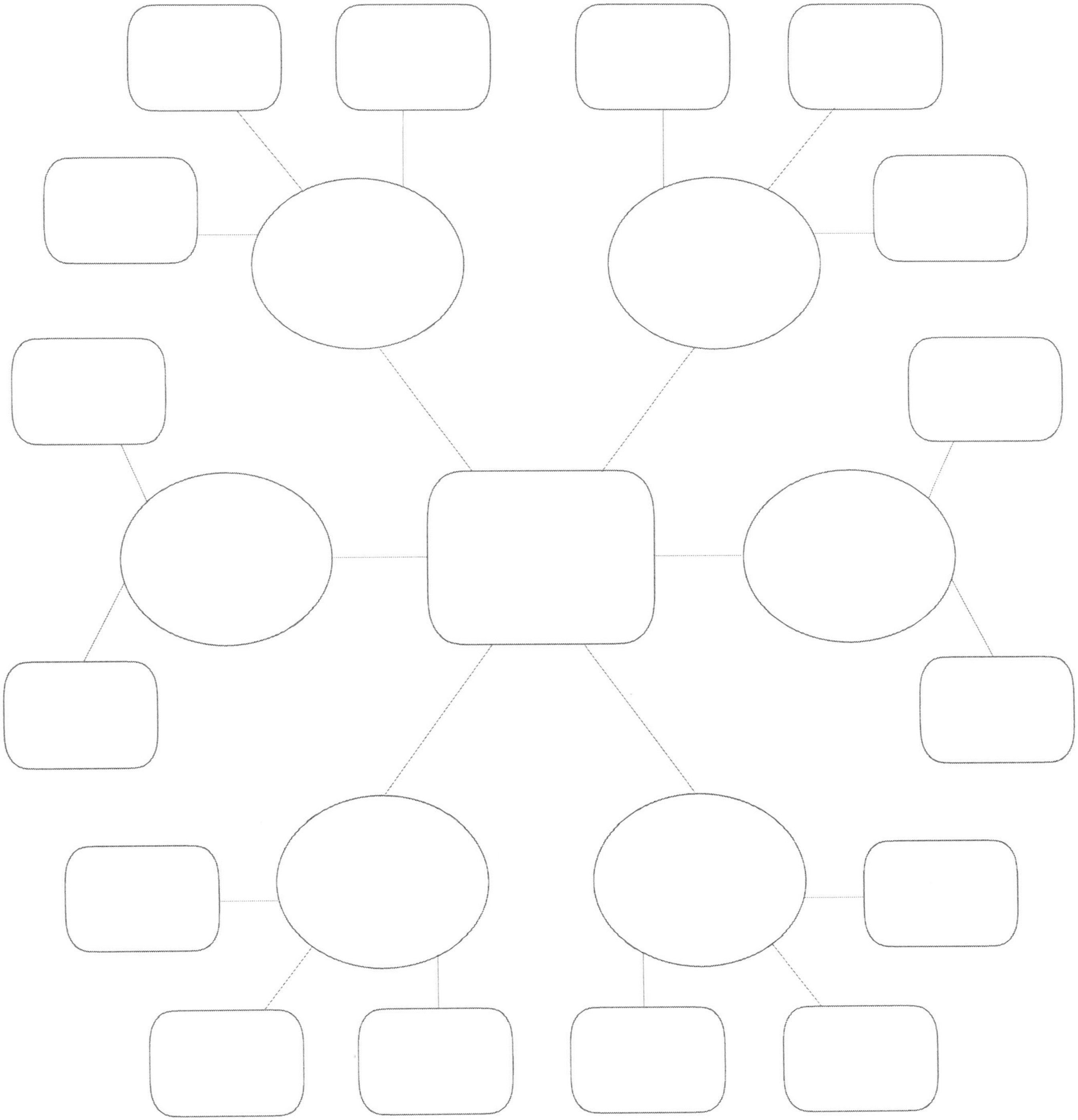

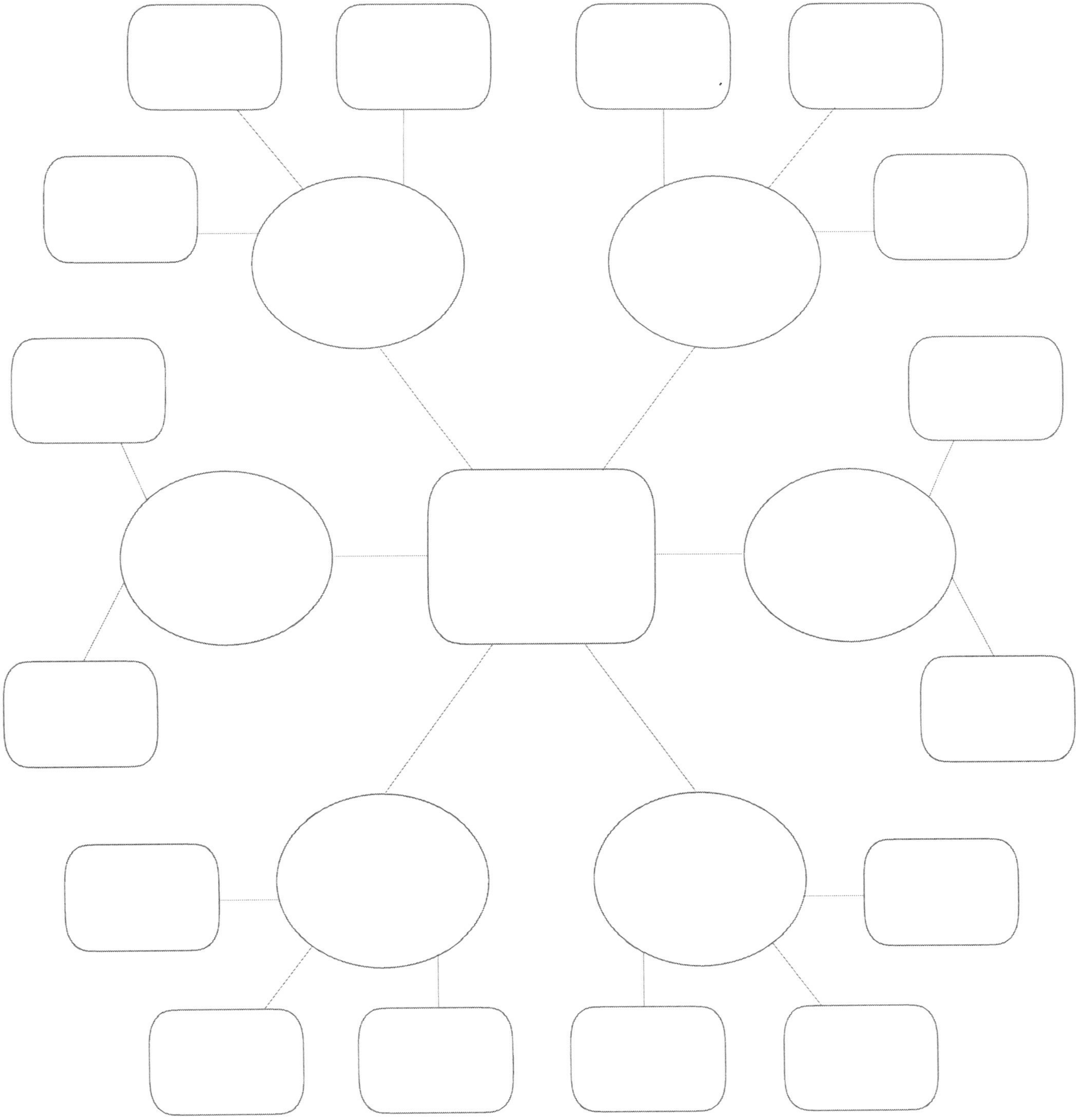

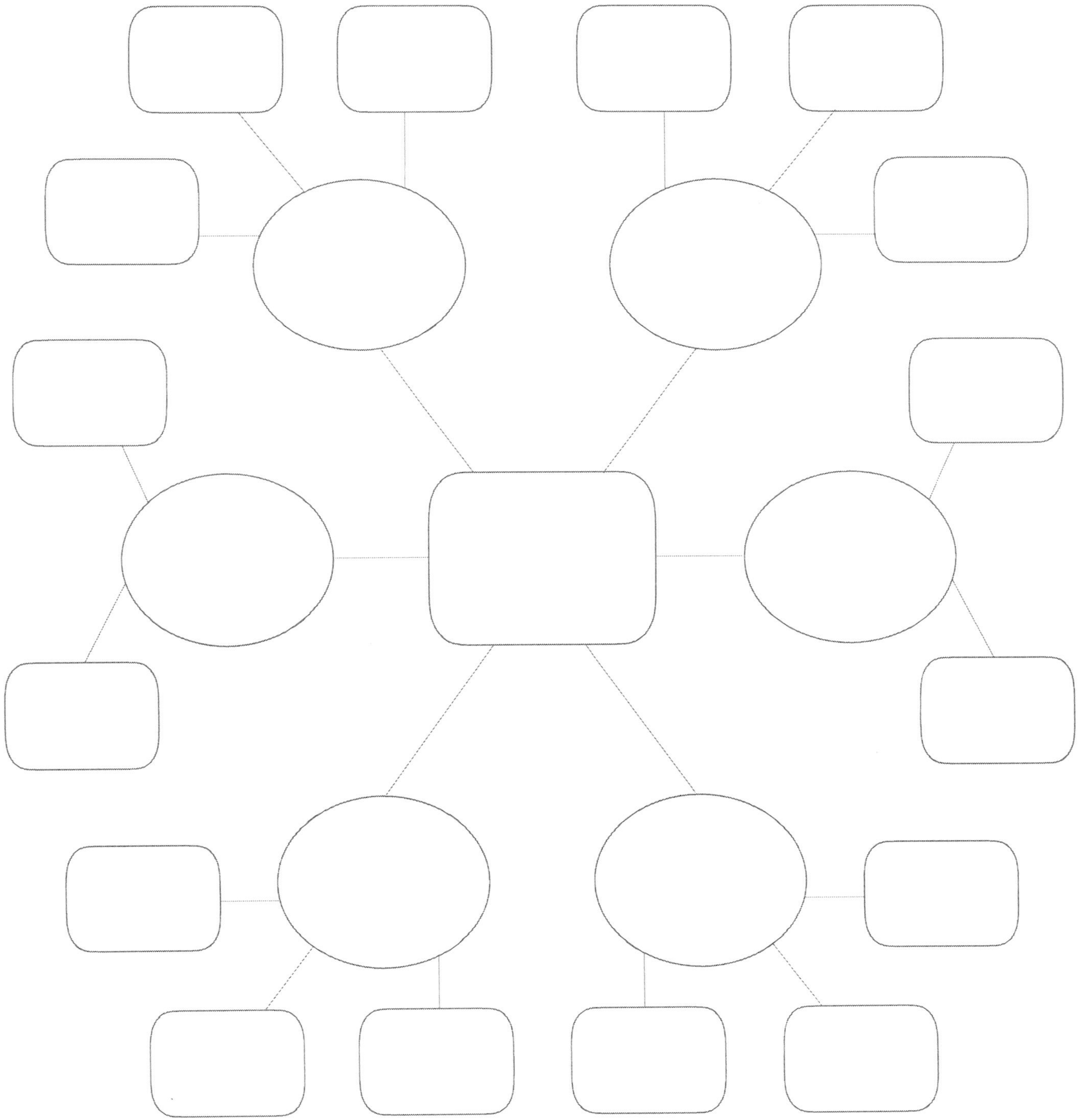

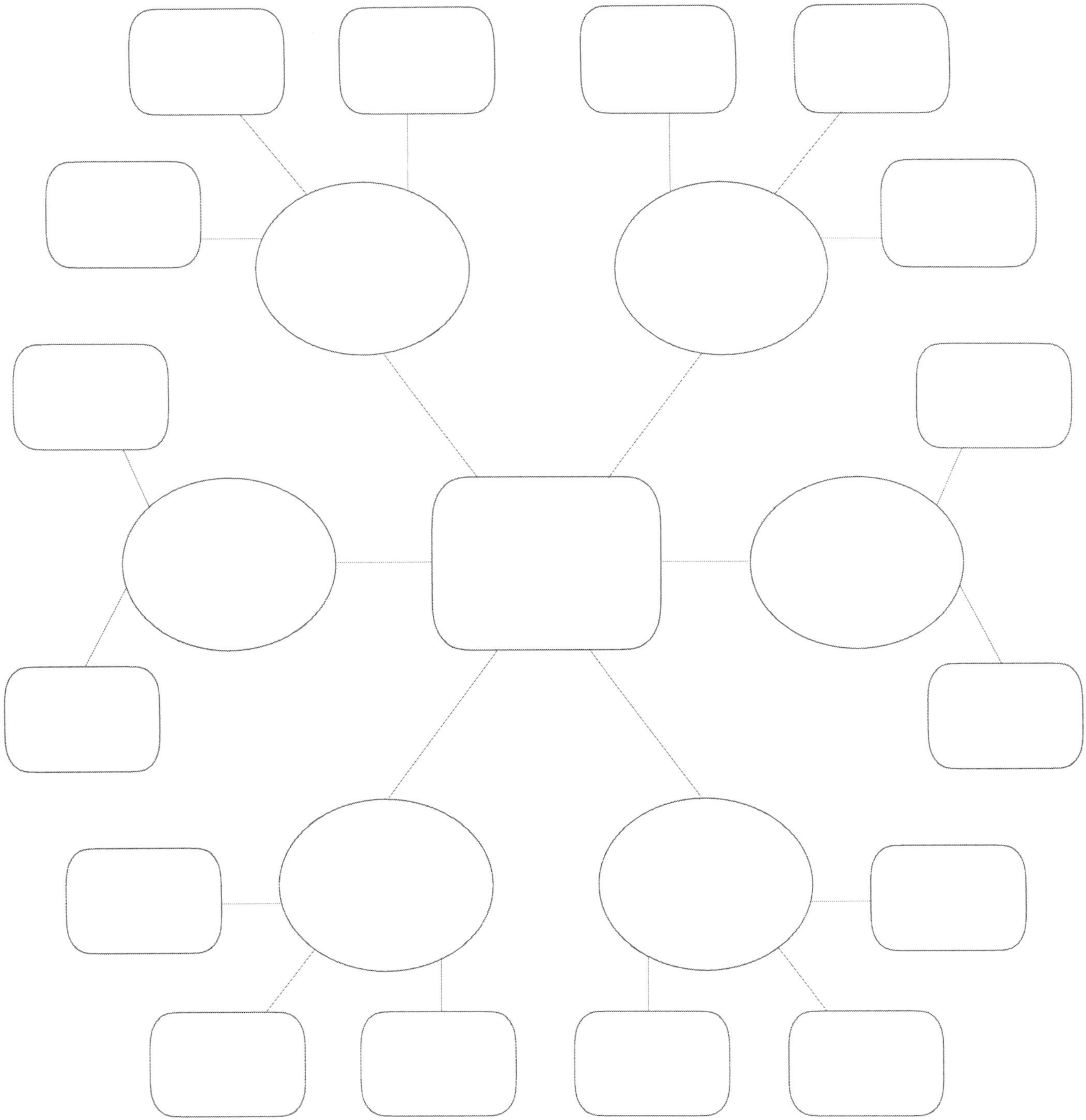

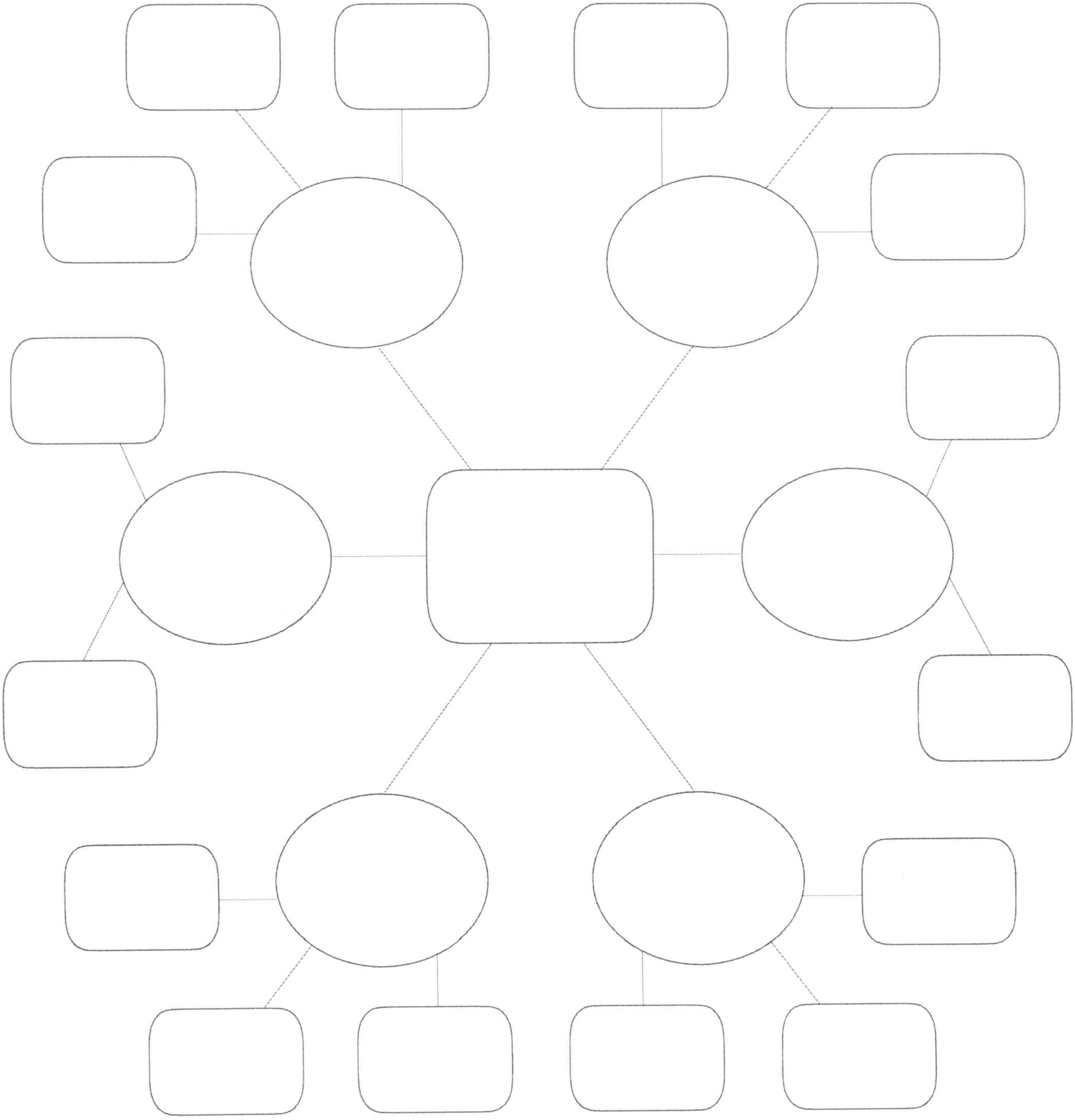

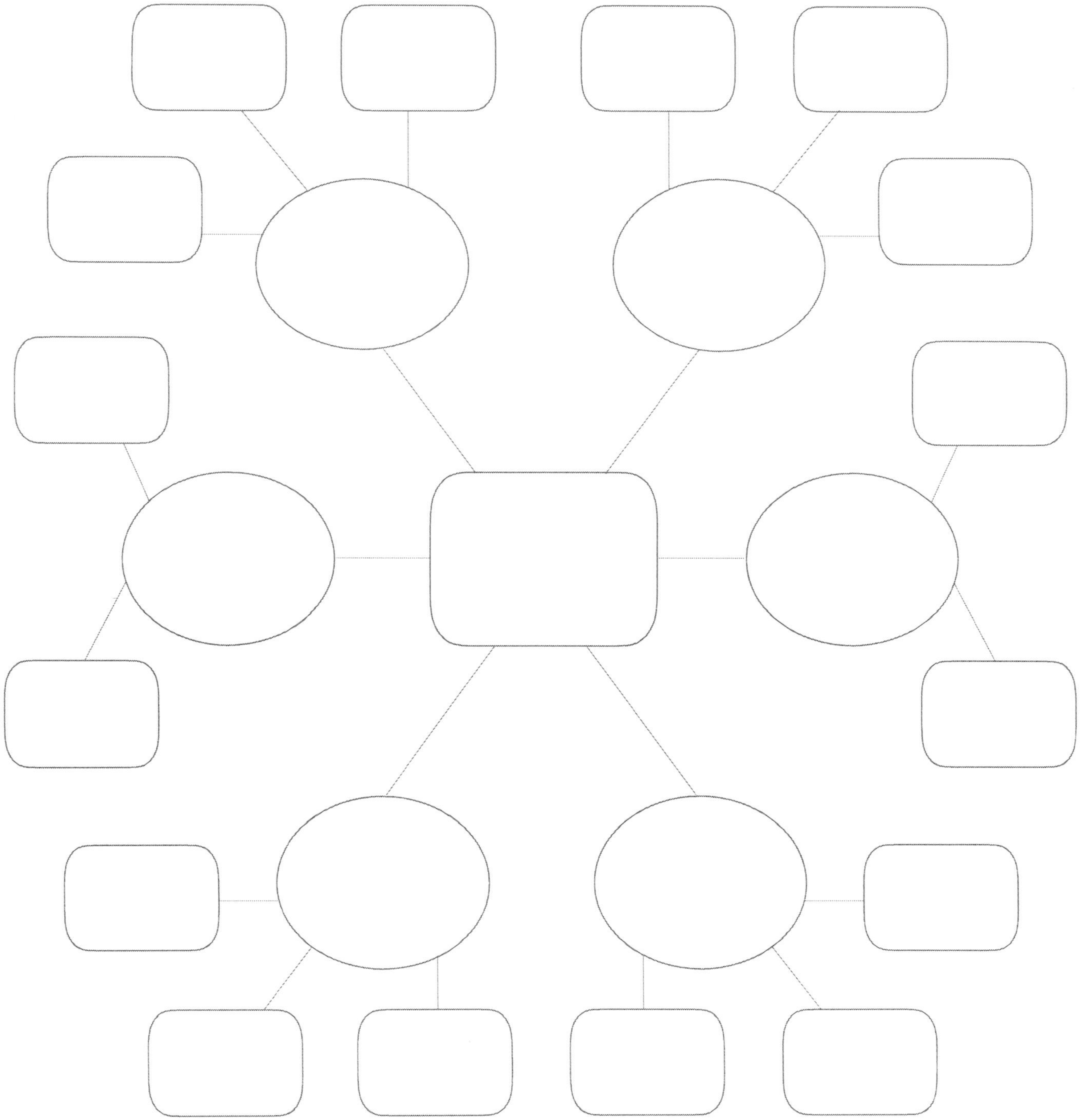